# Deep, Blue Odds

# Deep, Blue Odds

Poems

## Lane Falcon

Sheila-Na-Gig Editions

ISBN: 978-1-962405-54-6
Library of Congress Control Number: 2026930120

Sheila-Na-Gig Editions
Russell, KY
Hayley Mitchell Haugen, Editor
www.sheilanagigblog.com

# Acknowledgments

Poems from *Deep, Blue Odds* have been published in

*American Poetry Journal*: "Glitter"
*The Carolina Quarterly*: "Rehearsal"
*The Chattahoochee Review*: "Lightness"
*Cream City Review*: "The Window"
*Harbor Review*: "Three Weeks"
*The Healing Muse*: "Escape from Cincinnati"
*The Journal*: "Oz"
*Mayday Magazine*: "Warrior"
*Medical Literary Messenger*: "Endoscope," "Exile"
*Medmic*: "After Decannulation" (Reprinted), "Blue Baby"
    (Reprinted), "Lightness" (Reprinted), "Merrily"
*New York Quarterly*: "New Year's Day," "Odds"
*Pawling Magazine*: "Trach Care" (Reprinted)
*Poet Lore*: "Stanchions"
*Poetry South*: "Affliction," "Rumpelstiltskin"
*Presence*: "At Ronald McDonald House"
*Rust & Moth*: "After Decannulation"
*Sheila-Na-Gig online*: "Learning to Swim," "Voice"
*Spoon River Poetry Review*: "Hospital Series"
*Stirring*: "The Good Doctor," "Trach Care"
*Swwim Everyday*: "The Center"
*Tar River Poetry*: "Interlude, with Daughter," "For Movement,"
    "Million Dollar Baby",
*Vita Poetica*: "Infinity's Ribcage"
*WWPH Writes*: "HIV Nightline"

# Contents

## Part 1: Odds

## Part 2: Our Lives Now

## Part 3: Hospital Series

## Part 4: Warrior

## Part 5: Learning to Swim

For my daughter and my son

*They threw you in and told you the rules and the first time they caught you off base they killed you.*

—Ernest Hemmingway, *A Farewell to Arms*

*You are the one*
*Solid the spaces lean on, envious.*
*You are the baby in the barn.*

—Sylvia Plath, "Nick and the Candlestick"

# Part 1: Odds

# Three Weeks

*...more than one third of all child deaths occur*
*within the first month of life...*
    —World Health Organization

1.

Just a dirty trick
should he sink into the ether,

the slot he left open,
the finger-groove of air.

2.

I stare at the hairs on his head
surface current

under his moleskin scalp.
Parallel veins head for the same vanishing

behind one ear: escape,
for me too, seems possible

if I can gaze myself in.
Mine for the smallest unit of space

between his first dying skin cells,
between the first brief lashes that line

his wakeless eyes.

3.

My son
stitched to the sheet by tubes and tape,

into the embers by Versed and pain.
His vocal cords, the ENT confirmed—

after he fished in his throat for
an image to explain the cyanosis,

the cry casting gill-like shadows
in his clavicle—paralyzed.

Fire flattens to ash,
the life I saw flare just yesterday

in his eyes

                          *Is that a smile?*

retracts.


~


*I fold into rectangles*

*my dearest wish:*

*the disappearing alphabet*

*of what I can't say*

*the air says for me.*

# Lightness

Envy the nurses who lord over him like suns,
lift wires from his body and prop them

inches off the skin with upturned diapers,
who lift him, a bundle of grapes, to change

the pillowcase he sleeps on from Mickey Mouse
*Out to Play* to robots,

who hand me the old one to take home and wash.
If I were the nurse

who slides the thermometer across his forehead,
places a rolled hospital blanket

between his blue knees, if it were me
scanning the serial code on the plastic anklet

he wears, the one that matches mine,
before giving the sedative or painkiller,

the paralytic or diuretic,          if I poured
vial after vial of the breastmilk I pump

into the feeding bag— I would leave here at night.
I too would touch

with extreme lightness, as if parting
a giant's hair.

# Odds

I ask the milk that springs
with the suction of the pump      *one two three*

gaining momentum then stopping
          road signs, counting odds and evens

how I counted cracks to foretell my mother's
fate
                    *Will he live?*


                                        Don't hedge the bet


it will kill you      to lose.

# Interlude, with Daughter

At Cox Farm, the cows lie by the fence,
the black one lifting her forehead

while I trace the spiral of fur between her eyes.
My 2-year-old daughter arrives at my shoulder

and reaches between the iron bars of the gate
to touch this dust-covered vault of a mammal.

Our hands pass amorphous human worry
into the cowlick where the fur begins—and again

what looks back at me is the boundary I crossed,
the curtain of my son's body, the moment

the doctor first pulled out the endoscope, said
*This is making me very nervous.*

What presents itself is the film, the membrane
separating word and meaning—how I stare

at the curtain in his hospital room, a prism
of multicolored squares: *Cheery*, I think,

despite knowing better, then, *I'm not really here
am I? This isn't a curtain, but a symbol for something else.*

# Endoscope

At the end of his third week,
his eyes wouldn't latch onto mine,
but he sucked as if he could climb
milk into this world, oxygen.
He fooled me and didn't.
That night in the car seat, his head
jerked one, two, three times
to the right, the shallow flapping
of a pinned leaf, the sudden grunt
that wouldn't let me sleep.
I couldn't understand the cry
from behind the closed door
of his throat. On Tuesday,
I set him in the baby bath
and laid the warm rag on his
chest—when he cried, his eyes
swam under the lids. *Dusky,*
the nurse practitioner said.
A cloud rose from some inner
plexus, colored his jaw and lips.
*Hypoxic,* the ENT said, then
unsnapped the onesie and pointed
at the shadows between his ribs,
the bats in his clavicle. Then we rushed,
my mother, the doctor and me,
into a room where I held him still
and wept as the doctor thread
the tiny camera around his septum,
down into his throat.

# Million Dollar Baby

My father thinks it's cruel to hook a baby up to machines;
to intubate and prowl for lesions is to scrape the face of the moon.

He loves that movie: Clint Eastwood and the boxer who bites off
her own tongue wanting to bleed to death

after being knocked into a neurological trench. No rules—
but who can look into the hole in my newborn's neck if I can't?

# Oz

Me in the world of machines—
here he is *doing great,* he is *doing awesome*
and an ENT I didn't know three weeks ago
stands at his head, the god of his stoma,
immaculate hole I will curve into
maybe four years, *maybe forever,* and all I can think
is how everything resembles a penis, even more
than his penis, the root-beer color of his scrotum,
the same color of my nipples, his father's lips,
which I don't remember from the base
of this kaleidoscope, where I twirl toward dirt,
Dorothy in the poppies.

# For Movement

To the patron saint of miracles
manifest in infants,

of the smallest piece, turning the pin
half a millimeter to the right,

bent music box spring or key
for a girl's diary—

this is my prayer, a sliver of wind
I send to a sacred box

only the smallest turn unlocks.

# Exile

It takes two nurses to push
the recliner closer to his crib

on the side where the ventilator
feeds breath after xeroxed breath

into his lungs, then lift him,
one holding the six-foot plastic

oxygen limb while the other
places him in the spindly

cradle of my arms. This is how
I come back into myself:

his skin chafed by hospital air,
angry-red, his head the size

of a crochet ball balanced
on the crook of my elbow.

So many things wrong with me
implode in his eyes,

his mouth opens, emits a cry
no one hears. He arrives

in a mold too small to hold
this cosmic injury,

and looks at me to meet him,
to bleed.

## Stanchions

I remember the look in his eyes
like the atmosphere was unkind,

he couldn't find his gills and was gathered
against the vent to that other world.

I stood between him and that world:
the feverish nursing (*how did he climb*

*that rope into my arms?*) Then came the hospital,
the doctors I let take him, save him

when milk and human touch could not.
I almost killed him, my denial,

chased him back into the slot he slipped
through, into the arms of angels

who stood at their stanchions, awaiting
the fruit of my hubris.

*Thank God for the doctors*
I should say, but it's stuck in my chest

like I swallowed a quarter
my throat can't forget.

# The Good Doctor

I walk out from
the wood floor where I've lain,

mirror tilted back in a film
of dust, empty bassinet—and under

a clamor of women's voices
I lose you.

I dream you tell me:
*Backtrack.* The shutter lifts

and your crisp, blue intelligence
grips, one last time,

the handle of my grief.

# Part 2: Our Lives Now

## Stoma

More than the buzz of machines,
the bell of the pulse-ox, the steam

and latex gloves, the day nurse and night
nurse separate us.

What comes from behind
his eyes, circles its den then retreats

before I can feed it.

# Channeling

*After the PICU*

With every task,
I stitch him

into this world,
fasten the tape

on the front of his diaper,
wrap and throw away,

with every lift
onto my shoulder,

clockwise circle
on his stomach

to quell the gas,
when I smooth

the hairs on his head,
with every button

I unsnap—
        I summon

the weight of every
*Why?*

I can't surrender:
*Arrive*

*at my fingertips.*
*Make him stay.*

## Trach Care

Baby blanket rolled under his shoulders
so his head drops back, he exposes

his neck, the tulip of the tracheostomy tube,
the split of gauze I fit under

the neonate rubber collar damp
with milk.    No one should have to endure

the constant bearing of his throat,
this hole *(I can't let close)*.

I pinch the plastic stem so it won't shift,
wipe away stickiness, dry and replace

with fresh gauze *(to prevent breakdown)*,
this new ritual less than five minutes.

And he sleeps:
a kind of forgiveness.

# Glitter

Dec. 6, my mother worries
the glitter will kill us all.

It spreads from the roll
of red and gold piped tree ribbon

to our hands, my daughter's cheek,
the hard plastic "o"

of my son's trach.
She remembers 7th grade:

I blew on a hubcap
and the tiniest shard of metal

flew into my cornea.
*I had to use these,* she says,

and holds up a pair of
pliers—

she's talking about
something else.

# Anhedonia, Springfield Mall

My daughter and I ride the kiddie train
past Direct Furniture, JC Penny's faceless

mannequins on display,
and I remember that dream, my son's neck

slips underwater and his face begins to close
how the hospitalist said his stoma would

in 15 seconds if the trach falls out.
But I'm here for her, with her blue beard

and panda eyes, a face strep
recently entered: sick season,

daycare five days a week so I can work
and her brother sleep to the lull of his nurse's Krio.

Then she sees the other rides, a spaceship
and ice cream truck, kids climbing

into acrylic saddles, screaming,
or strapped into carts fashioned like firetrucks

we somehow missed at the entrance.
And I wonder if this loop ever ends—

what if now, in and of itself, is
the turning?

## Blue Baby

Lips blue, face licorice blue,
my mouth, soft rectangular lateral
blue, him in his racecar pajamas blue,
blue about to burst, blue buried
in chalky glass. The night nurse says
*He's turning blue* as if to correct me.
We're in my apartment, a minute or two
after the first cry woke, tolled three four
times in a row for me—*I sat on the toilet*
*until the last drop fell       four five six—*
blue and his hands cool. Hours before,
he smiled through the bars of the crib,
bolstered by hands, a new-trick blue.
*That baby, this baby,* air spliced in his throat,
the blue of lungs, crustacean blood,
diluted Slurpee, popsicle passed through
the ice cream truck window, lips dyed
by a Tootsie-Pop fucking blue. His eyes
roll back as his brain floods with oxygen.
I hold the emergency trach in the stoma,
balloon to the nozzle of the tank as it blooms
with helium. His eyes give, come back
and take away—Capricorn moon
or strangulation blue. His cheek still cool,
where blue rested, blew away.

# The Persuasions

*Day of conception*

If there was ever a chance
he wouldn't ignite—

a still transparent seed—
clear the closing

door into existence,
unable to discern

the shape, the voices
of four men singing acapella

in the hospice where I worked
vanquished it.

He heard the road
he traveled paved

by assonance—
and if there was a chance

he didn't hear, asleep
in that pre-nascent moment,

their voices sung him into spirit:
*Oh* quickening

of mirage air,
*Oh* atmosphere

through waves of clear
before the flame.

## Bedtime Story

No parameters, poles through which
meandering muscles are guided,

but my daughter is always there with Soda-Pop,
her imaginary horse—a butler or father—

a castle blurred in the background.
The more tired I am, the more bizarre:

notary publics appear. And she knows
when the end comes too soon, truncates the diffuse

non-plot. Not yet three, I owe her this hour
before sleep. As the world outside her bedroom

door shapeshifts—the night nurse arriving,
switching on my son's oxygen-infused

humidifier—the story expands.
Soda-Pop knows what she needs

how a constable knows the look of
a good lunch counter,

how a city knows the robbers in its alleys,
the knocked-over garbage cans,

the smell of stockyards gushing
through it veins.

# The Women

Little boy in my arms
like his father,

who exuded,
through the barbed wire wrap

of his circumstances,
the same oblivion.

I have my daughter
at my side at 3 am,

oldest love aligned
with dusty ribs,

my mother who still
spits their father's name

like fiberglass—
they are the ones

who will fight for me,
who lay themselves,

strips of dipped gauze,
over my broken hope.

## Our Lives Now

Revolve around killing
whatever chooses him

as a host: tracheitis or,
this time, thrush.

My mother primes the table,
the waffled sanitary sheet

from an open trach kit,
a stack of drain sponges

she couldn't throw away—
*100% cotton!*—

even after she heard
they make it worse,

draw bacteria to the stoma
we'd die to protect.

But before I can descend
onto his mouth

for the fifteenth time today,
to wipe away

the lace along his gums,
inside his cheek,

I find her in my bedroom,
head in her hands:

*The things we do to him.*
I can't pause,

can't ask when he'll speak—
he finds me wherever I go,

waits outside the bathroom
door, his thin shadow,

the rattle of his trach,
the amplified passage

of phlegm in his throat.
The gentian violet

dyes us all: rub with sugar
and olive oil, wash

with baby soap, repeat
until only a shadow

remains. The rest sheds
with every movement

of his mouth it seems,
as his lips open and close,

with every muted
scream.

# Rehearsal

*For my son, who still can't speak*

Pans on the kitchen floor, small to big
he stacks inside the Dutch oven.

He masters this, unstacks, one by one,
a clang-bang cacophony, corners

of a cracked language.
He doesn't flinch, doesn't slam the cabinet door,

the window wide to the element
of his making, his senses,

floor-deep with noise.

# Part 3: Hospital Series

*When your ways are beyond my understanding,*
*I will adore you in silent trust.*

—St. Ignatius of Antioch
(written on a Post-it by a woman at the family services
desk, Cincinnati Children's Hospital)

# The Window

*Laryngotracheal Reconstruction 1*

My daughter wringing wind out of the cat tail weeds,
*Go away,* she says, the crisp ends limpid

over the flowerbox hedge, then, *I can be a superhero
and get my brother.*

On the way to the restaurant,
*He's okay,* the flipside of sibling rivalry

glistens with a pinkness I don't want to touch.
*I make you sad,* she says, coming closer, looking away

and I tell myself it's okay to cry right here
over pinot grigio and a basket of fries,

the beefy chicken tenders she surprised me
by liking, then it's not. *Smile,*

the brochure at the hospital said,
*it makes your child calm,*

but the next morning I feel guilty for falling
asleep while she played a video game.

And the hotel room gives no comfort.
And we're living inside an eye—

the cornea receiving dull,
morning light.

# Hospital Series

## *Laryngotracheal Reconstruction 2*

*Pre-op*

What kind of woman—that's the easiest question—
hands her son to a team of gentle aliens,

a praying mantis in a surgical mask
and light-deflecting lenses
                              *Hey little man.*

I can't curse the surgeons because
I'm the one who wanted this, fed him well the night before

to fatten the ribcage they break into. Afterwards,
they offer him, this ball of suffering child,

the neck stitch hidden by gauze: here he is,
sedated and beautiful, the quiet line

of his eyelashes.
*In silent trust—*

*Intubation*

My son sleeps
in the hospital bed,

a tube taped
to his cheek, and coiled

at his feet, a wreath
of tubes.

Gauze on his neck
reflects a blinking

light, the stoma,
stitches and drain

fastened, sedation,
a blanket he fought

then let in,
let warm him.

*Stirring (Day 10 Post-op)*

Affixed into the code, the vault
with its weighted door and

letters etched on buttons
   *abc, cdf,*

as methadone blurs
the room around him.

Blood dries where the tape edge
rubs his cheek,

patches of adhesive
on his chest and foot.

And maybe
it's the knock of my voice—

not my voice but its inflection—
a riddle he knows the answer to,

a song he sings to the next phrase
even before it's there.

*Extubation*


Pulmonary effusion, entitles,
the carbon monoxide

he won't let go
builds mountains,

invisible capes on his lungs.
The attending asks if he's ever

breathed on his own.
The last time I saw him

without a tube in his throat,
canula curved

into sacred tracheal flesh,
he was three weeks old—

*What happens inside his body?*

*Stridor*


3 a.m., the hitch
in his breath reels me

from the surface of sleep.
The music retracts,

the strings of the instrument
over the open lobe,

hooked onto by danger
or treasure. *He's smiling,*

my mother says
but he sounds worse.

No grip can be found
to tune his breathing.

*Day 18 Post-op*


Three rooms wave between us,
a flag we can't center or grip—

my militance and his caprice,
the wind another factor.

Three things could happen,
and the doctor won't say chance of recovery,

even after seven surgeries, the shield
of anesthesia protecting him

from arrows of pain or fear.
I've heard it said:

time is the only way to measure
the universe. It's no retractable ruler,

time—I can't get back the loops
I've given over.

*Day 30 Post-op*


Tonight, I pray
from an absence of faith—

every instrument depends
on some hollow,

and hollows yield beauty
when contained.   Tonight,

I pray with someone
else's faith, someone who

doesn't exist—expose
her body, that shallow,

white shelf wiped clean
then dirty again.

Tonight, I pray a chain
of paper men—a chariot

that hangs, God-garland,
from my hands.

*Week 6*


So much asymmetry
overlapping—

frequency of thought,
my worry coded

in soundwaves. The seesaw
of his breath,

the sucking-in of clavicle,
the eking out,

a rosary of shadows
I want to lift from around

his neck, his memory
of ever wearing it.

*Rm. 506*

I imagine I climb a ladder and pull the attic door open, crawl
onto the ledge, stand, the cotton-candy fiberglass crunching
under my feet, the dust it coughs up.

Is this how it feels not to breathe?

My lack of context shames me. I want to breathe his bastard air,
hole in his oxygen,

want to know what spaghetti loop he culls the atoms from
to keep alive.

I want to water that garden, grow his sustenance and funnel
it into this dishpan room.

Weeks in a hospital in a run-down city.

*Re-trached*


His head, like a hat, swings
on the tip of a cane, the new trach

too long, his eyes too heavy
to lift from the floor.

      The problem with hospital room projections,
him and I—the ends

of this misery—I wake and can't exhale
the defeat.

      I heard him cry,
cough, his truncated *mama*

just days ago—
his voice, a snapped string

of pearls he trailed around
the room. God,

I never wagered so much on a word:

                  *mama*

                           *ma*

*ma*     *mama*

*Swansong*

Imagine a life,
bent over a caterpillar

inching its way across
the bike path,

the millions of mocha
strands of fur,

coagulated, combed
to untouchable fluff.

I listen to him grunt
when he breathes,

numbers on the monitor
bleat and blink.

Only I know
his rhythm, deeper

when he sleeps,
as his breath slides

along its continuum.
And if it takes my whole life,

I'll guard his song.
I'll wait for him.

# Part 4: Warrior

# Infinity's Ricage

My daughter asks if there's a second
sky,

one in heaven this time,

arched above earth's
opera house marble ceiling.

She wants to know the physical, I expect, limits
of overlapping orbs, arches perfected.

She wants to know
what protects us.

# New Year's Day

The cold clamped down, the heat turned off, or turned on and the car doors open as I scrambled back and forth to wet rags, rinse them of vomit while my mother dug a fresh outfit for him from a packed suitcase. What it was that month—why he wouldn't eat and vomited so violently—was that the trach was too long and scraped the back of his throat. I remember realizing he'd thrown up again as my mother turned the key and we backed out of the rental's driveway, after the dreaded packing-up and feigning goodbye to a three-day vacation in Williamsburg, through which I struggled as I struggled through everything that year, trying to be happy and not, trying to buoy myself with gratitude. The sound of him retching and then the stripping bare, the bagging of vomit rags and clothes. The changing, bundling, cleaning under the trach ties, twisting my body into the back seat to recreate the warmth, satiety he lost. I remember the calm of finally leaving, still arrested by the freeze and frenzy, how my son, limp, not even crying, stared out the window, had let me change him.

# HIV Nightline, San Francisco 2002

I volunteered to listen—the voice
on the other end sometimes

a spool of night unraveling,
some poor mother's son who said he deserved it

or a "manic-depressive" in a phone booth
in Chicago: *I got to go*

*to another phone.* Some nights,
the red light blinked as someone tried to call,

call again, and I couldn't pause
another crying
                              long enough

to even ask them to hold.
I wanted to help, from the safe side

of the screen, I wanted their pain
to immunize me. Even then

I knew it was pure lottery.

# Survival

The tube in my son's neck he scratches
the reddened skin around,

the soul's arrow sired by what
I've done wrong. The psychiatrist flashes

his logic: *not the case,* he says, *primordial,*
*superstition*—but helplessness feels worse,

a silk-greedy elf with teeth long as
sewing needles I've bartered my sanity

to dissuade. *These are the things*
*we can control. These are the things we can't.*

# The Science of Breathing

The mind follows the breath,
one area in the brain flies the kite

of respiration, the genetic fist,
a function regenerated in mammals,

a rhythm dropped in utero
like a needle on vinyl.

How do you know,
in the greyscale world of the medulla,

where apnea lives, an infant's death
in sleep, the functional blink

that stays closed,
the letting go?

# The Shield

In that nightmare, I'm never safe—
my son dies

to teach me that lesson,
the life knuckled from him with one

last cough.      When does it go
away—this fear

he won't stay with me,
a stem rooted in me

      yanked out?
And I turn to my daughter:

when this happens,
if this happens,

      *Will you be the night*
*I wrap myself in*

*if the stars choke*
*on their own light?*

# Affliction

Sometimes, a current moves through him laterally,

lifts the left arm to enter through the palm
and arrest the limb.

Some silver ball of light pings off his bones
then out through the other side.

The neurologist says *abnormal*
and I dog-ear

deep into the night watching videos of children seizing,
then drive to work the next morning, my vision shaking:

*When does the bad news end?*

# Rumpelstiltskin

I've been praying for a sign,
I've been hammering my meat-thunk hands

into the blue, the keys rebounding off the wall
where they're nailed. I've been nailing my dreams,

satchels of clouds, to the wall's boards.
Hope is the house I live in, and die in,

the mice hang by their tails, the red eyes gleaming
hatred, the shrieking

dying decapitated entrails of hope. The slipping
on and falling over,

the slog in the dust, the crap shoot,
the heel slick, sliding down,

the breaking of bones on the stairs.
I've been hoping and strained,

and the cotton-candy webs
you think you can walk through—

they stick to you.

# Escape from Cincinnati

I still haven't gone back to that place—the vacuousness
I felt while they dripped fentanyl into my son's bloodstream

after his second failed reconstruction surgery. How I'd go
on a panicked run every morning in a city where opioids reigned,

where a man fell to his knees, a woman froze under the overpass.
In the waiting room, a grandmother cried, her daughter

just dead from overdose, her grandson just waking
from general anesthesia. How fucked-up it felt

that night when I begged the nurse to give him more,
enough to sustain him, dull his pain and mine,

his pupils blooming with fear when he started to wake.
How small a measure they lent. How small the graces we get

when we're rowing in grief.

# Whatever the Cost

The doctor tells my daughter to breathe
big balloons, blow out the bad

as if it were bubblegum,
as if walls could contain it.

My sister suggests I slide an egg
over her eyelids,

down the centerline of her skull,
vacuum the thoughts through the shell

and into the unborn yolk, then crack
in ceremony and let soak: uselessness.

My daughter tells me why in loose change—:

*I wish it were just you*
*and me. I hate my brain.—*

I don't know the worth of,
from a country I can't travel to.

But I'd barter my body if it led her home,
lay myself down if I could be her path,

the trail between unmovable rocks,
the foothold in sliding dust.

# Warrior

Wires stream from his scalp—all the primary
colors like the tracks of the toy maze in the intake office

he pushed each wooden bead along, talking,
smiling when the woman behind the desk

snuck him two Hot Wheels cars, when he walked
against my warning to her knees. Now the EEG tech

wraps his head in gauze, guides the tangle of wires
though a sleeve that hangs down his back. This

will be his burden for the next ten hours, at his side
while he sleeps, the ends feeding the machine's

giant cord. *Tonight, you're a superhero*, the tech says,
but he won't look up. It scares me, this new stoicism,

the not letting me touch him when mummified again
by medicine and its machines. Even when I wrap

him in his favorite blanket, lift his saddled head and lay
it on his home pillow, he doesn't look at me.

He barely moves. The common betrayal of the life he loves,
he swallows.

## The Center

Bridges keep collapsing
in his body.

What if the graft dissolves
like last time?

Like the surgery didn't
happen?

Then weeks of epinephrine,
choking so bad

he shot up in his crib
to grab me,

and panic wicked him away
shit after shit,

vomit after vomit.
Every day, death peered closer,

until I let go, let them
replace the trach.

This time, they'll cut
the graft wider, place it higher,

so when I uncurl the canula
from the scar-twined

hole in his neck—
and in his eyes,

a single leaf of trust
floats in the fear—

he will breathe.
It will hold.

# Part 5: Learning to Swim

# Voice

Cincinnati again on the horizon.
In another month,

the third surgery with
the esteemed wizard of airway

dynamics: the propulsion,
the sculpting of vocal wings—

the same friction that creates
lift. One more month, and me,

my son, and a caravan
of suitcases will embark on

the ninth leg of this journey,
the filters he coughs

off his trach landing in the path
of strangers who arrive before us

*Do you need this?*
What they really want to know,

what we all want to know,
is *Why?*     One more month,

and we'll check in at the same
hotel we always do,

and while we wait in the lobby
for the Medicaid authorization

to click, he'll act more alive
than ever, as if

performing for all
the recalibrating minds

of strangers. One more month.
Still, I wait for a sign:

this time his airway is ready,
for faith to rise

from the asphalt
of my heart.

## The Day I Leave with Her Brother, Laryngotracheal Reconstruction 3

She knows I'll return and she knows
some things won't.

Like the wall she's felt blindly for
four years now,

since I went to the bathroom
to pee on a stick and returned crying.

Like the father she doesn't know
who doesn't answer his phone when she calls.

Like the boyfriend, over every night,
then not.

Even Ani, the fellow sibling she met
at Ronald McDonald House

the last time I bet our lives on a chance
for "normal."

They roamed the halls, feral for weeks,
while Ani's brother healed

and I cried at my son's
bedside across the street—

*Sometimes we just fail.*

# The Caterpillar

*For my daughter, walking back from Cincinnati Zoo*

Much of life you trudge from one station to the next,
despite the heat and incline,

the steaming sidewalk outside the hospital,
a part of your body broken—

how your brother, a sliver of his right rib
spacing his vocal cords, a tube thread through his septum,

wakes in the room and winces.
How your mother, who would gladly claim it,

trach and all—post her useless flag in roaming pain—
eats, sleeps and runs in the shadow of a mass

no one sees. How your grandma
drives to the apartment every morning—

her swollen ankle pumping the gas,
her partial blindness—to reorder kitchen chaos,

close the cabinets fury flies open.
Every day, my dear, we inch somewhere

that may or may not be worth the pain
of pushing. We force ourselves forward, gut first.

# Merrily

Trach safely above the bathwater,
the bubbles flattened, lukewarm, he sings

*wo wo wo ye bo,* the skin sealing the space
around the tube how the PICU nurse told me it would

years earlier—*He can swim, sing, anything*—
and, in that moment, I didn't believe her but,

lulled by the worn denim of her voice,
her sitting down to talk to me *off the record,*

let myself relax how now, knowing still
the danger, I watch him pour water

from the helm of his plastic boat,
and the words scratch past his vocal cords

which still don't open, the frozen pistol of a flower,
all stalk, no bloom, the iron lattice melody,

his voice, a softer green    I've listened
to so long, I understand.

# And Yet, And Yet

1.

Would I feel better
if Sinatra had sung for me,

if Mercer had written, under
his whiskey rainbow, my ruby-

slipper remorse, or if all the men
of Motown had bowed, in powder blue,

to shower me, little woman,
with their devotion?

      Maybe then I wouldn't feel
this fire hydrant opening, this rock hard

and solvable gap, this channel to
the underground, this sap,

the sewer's jewel brown,
this refuge for rats and homeless,

this moon crater, this loneliness?

2.

I've been wanting to write a poem
about my daughter's hair,

but haven't found the time or container
to compare

the living strands that leap
under the beam of my early-morning flashlight

after reading an email from
her kindergarten teacher about rampant lice.

The mink-brown too, alive,
I realize: quicksilver shine

slips and leaps as she giggles and lurches
from the pillow,

her hair an extension of how
neurons keep firing

in spite of pain,
how dreams bud wings

and stretch long
untenable legs—

# After Decannulation

There will always be one
who pulls you to the edge

by the neck—his happiness,
a trophy I hold

by the neck and champion
above my head.

The child I hold closer,
his skin still slick,

this boy I fished
from the deep, blue odds,

who I kept whole,
and breathing.

## Crossing the Street

We return home, and it feels
like this time, for real,

it's over, the last trach,
the collar the size

of a man's wrist, ziplocked
in a bag I still keep

with me, a band-aid
over the stoma I'd dive

in front of a truck to protect.
Every day, though, it closes

more—and I'm supposed
to just let go the fear,

earth opening to swallow
me and my children, move

from the ledge of the gaping
wound that fate,

or God, or pure human will
coughed us from

the depth of, still whole,
still holding hands.

# Grace Song

And sometimes, this apartment feels sacred—
mother, daughter, son—as if God leans in

for a closer look.
The counters must be clean, the carpet vacuumed,

coffee stains blended by the right light.
Often at night,

the three of us playing school in the walk-in closet,
my daughter teaching. Or in pajamas

piled on the couch
and there:

God's elongated shadow shelters us as we inch
home from wandering, how I lean

into my children's sleeping ears:
*You are beautiful. You are wonderful. You are loved.*

# Music Box

And should,
at 3 am, the barrel,

pins and comb
his life leans on

dissolve into
the music

of his body,
I pray I'll know—

and that,
when he sleeps

in the room
next to mine,

God watches,
should I resign

to my body's
sinking cradle,

as notes tiptoe
by.

# At Ronald McDonald House

*Annual check-in*

Bless the ramp on the sidewalk where parents
push strollers with ventilators hanging off the back,

where once I lugged the go bag and suction machine
while my son slept, a tube in his nose and a fresh scar

across his rib. Bless the business center where I yelled
into my phone to the surgeon who wouldn't release

his notes, wouldn't bleed into the cracks of the misery
all his good intention had afflicted. Bless one more day

I don't need to rush my son to the ER across the street,
no surgery has failed, no waiting for the intern to ask

him questions he'll deflect to the absent attending.
Bless the bells that alarm, the laminated code blue

instructions in every room, the refrigerator where
parents store cold medicine. Bless the Reds mascot

who once leaned over my son's stroller and silently
held his hand. Bless the pilot who followed us

off the plane later to hand him a pin he let slide
to the side of his stroller with all the other prizes

he'd earned for his pain. Bless the ache in my neck,
the muscles bunched from waking all night, praying

to a god I didn't think watched my son's chest creak
in and out. Bless this house blooming with parents'

desperate prayers. And bless this sleeping boy—
*dear God, bless this boy*—who arrived

on the other side of this place, who has yet to hold
it in his hands, to feel the weight of it.

# Learning to Swim

Five years ago today,
you roiled inside me, breathed

your last full breaths,
unmitigated organism,

aquatic or otherwise,
in or outside my body.

When you arrived,
you breathed through a sliver

of space, a vestige
from our caveman days

when no other anecdote
existed to maintain

the living oxygen tank
of our bodies.

You were trached,
aspirated on liquids

until you trained
the defected flower

of your larynx to spill
safely what settled

in its grooves. You learned
this by yourself. Today,

at an outdated resort
in West Virginia, in the

outdoor pool, water unwinds
silken laps on your skin.

Your mouth, a little knot,
you hop forward,

then you see me and lunge,
grasp me so tight you'll drag

tracks with your fingernails.
I let you sink     *one*     *one thousand,*

*two   one thousand*       then
hook you in my arms.

A Special Thank You To:

The miracle-working Complex Airway Team at
Cincinnati Children's Hospital

My mother, father and sister: Always Faithful

# About the Author

Lane Falcon's poems have been published in *American Poetry Journal, The Carolina Quarterly, Cream City Review, Harbor Review, The Healing Muse, The Journal, Medmic, New York Quarterly, Ninth Letter, Poet Lore, Poetry South, Rhino, Quarter After Eight, Rust & Moth, Sheila-Na-Gig online, Spoon River Poetry Review, Swwim Everyday, Tar River Poetry*, and more. *Deep, Blue Odds,* was a finalist for the Black Lawrence Press Hudson Prize, and a semi-finalist for the 2022 Tupelo Press Berkshire Prize.

www.ingramcontent.com/pod-product-compliance
Lightning Source LLC
Chambersburg PA
CBHW030505130626
46549CB00007B/2865